MW00779421

BLUE COLORED MUSE

Blue Colored Muse

A poetry collection inspired by the pure beauty of the Great Lakes State and the talented artists who call it home.

JENNIFER GORDON

Jennifer Gordon Poetry

CONTENTS

AUTHOR'S NOTE

All of my life, I have been drawn to the arts. I look upon people with artistic talents as a child might admire the full harvest moon. There is something magical about the ability to bring an image up from the depths of your own imagination and present it to the rest of the world in a visual form that they can comprehend. I have never had this kind of talent. To be brutally honest, I find even a simple stick figure on paper to be a challenge. But somewhere along the line, I discovered the power of words. I fell in love with their ability to create a passionate form of artistic expression. And this is where I have found my home; in poetry. And yet, from the comfort of my home, I have continued to look out my window, ever in awe of painted landscapes and sculpted stone. And as I write, I often look to the world of visual art for works that stir my soul and inspire my heart.

Two years ago, I took to pairing my words with visual images on social media. I found joy in creating pairings where I felt the images not only brought the words to life, but where the words brought deeper meaning to the images as well. There was one photographer in particular whose work I was continually drawn to. In kindness, he often allowed me to layer my poetry on top of his photography, creating works that deeply connected with my readers. Somewhere in that time period, a seed was planted in my mind that eventually bloomed into the book you are holding.

I am a loyal native to my home state of Michigan, so much so that I have never desired to live anywhere else. I can think of nothing more beautiful to write about than the home I love and no greater way to enhance that writing than by finding inspiration from other artists who consider this their home as well. The artists featured in this book have graciously and generously allowed me to use their work as inspiration for each of the poems you will find in these pages. My hope is that you will admire these men and women as much as I do. I ask that you take your time in reading my words. Allow yourself to soak them in. Find beauty in the art before you. And most importantly, remember that life is an art form all its own, and the pursuit of inspiration is up to you.

(Sketch by Katie Emery)

The pleasant scent of petrichor
has made its way through May
but now I sense these days of rain
will soon begin to fade

Replaced by the hues of a burning June
and a sun whose reaching rays
will transform trees to a host of shade
as springtime slips away

(Painting by Shelby Kregel)

The world has
wanted me
to be so many things
But all I have ever
wanted to be
is free

(Photo by Joel Marotti)

How brilliant we humans
consider ourselves to be
And yet how often we fail to comprehend
so much of our surroundings

We are a natural creature
are we not?
And yet we find ourselves lost
amidst the wild

Unprepared
for the rawness of life
Uninspired
by the vastness of the sky

Lacking the tools we need to survive

How humbling it feels
to be in the presence of eagles
To witness a greatness
beyond our own

And if only for a moment
to fully understand
there are things of this world
more wondrous than man

(Photo by Joe Gall)

And like the flowers
of the fields
I will turn my face towards
the sun
Knowing the only way
to grow
is to look in the direction
I long to go

(Painting "Follow The Sun" by Andrea Rich)

I am peaceful
in the quietness of solitude
Connected
to the sense of calm
that gently laps
upon the shore

(Photo by Joel Marotti)

When I need to know
the truth of someone's character
I simply watch their interactions
with other creatures

For if a man
does not treat his animals well
there are parts of his heart
where weakness dwells

(Wood Burning by Angel Portice)

There is love in the distance
Always shifting
Waiting
Hanging in the atmosphere

There is love beyond measure
Hovering there
Somewhere
Folded into time itself

There is love without limits
Reaching out
Open palmed
Never far beyond the horizon

And somehow
Someday
I pray that you will find yourself
Immersed inside its light

(Painting "Evening Stroll Along The Pier" by Andrea Rich)

Some days
the weight of the world
is so heavy
that I break it apart in pieces
Haul it bit by bit
out into the forest
Hang it there
upon the branches
and ask the limbs of the earth
to bear the burdens
I can no longer carry

(Painting "Silence Is Golden" by Kathleen Kalinowski)

In those moments
of deepest silence
please know
I am not at a loss for words
I am simply so filled
with meaning
that the million words
beneath my tongue
are still deciding
whether they want
to stay or go

(Photo by Sara Wright)

There is nothing that soothes
a grieving soul
like a walk through the woods
holding hands with a ghost

(Painting "Firefly Evening" by Kathleen Kalinowski)

I could watch the setting
of the sun
for a million moments more

And I would never tire
of the notes it strums
upon my soul

(Photo by Matt Davis)

| 2 |

(Sketch by Katie Emery)

Paint me from the pallet
of an autumn scene
Drench my days
in the brilliant colors
put on display by the falling leaves

For the world has a way
of stealing joy
when we fail to pause and take the time
to observe the moments
we are meant to enjoy

And like the trees
we must accept
that sometimes beautiful things
will leave
Giving us reason to mourn and grieve

But for today
I will bask in the hues of a golden season
Reminding myself
that how I choose to spend my days
determines the course my life will take

(Painting by Shelby Kregel)

I often feel humbled
in nature
As if perhaps
I am unworthy of its beauty

As if I am an intruder
in a landscape made
for creatures with less demons
than I carry

(Photo by Joe Gall)

I sense the wisdom of the world
neatly packaged among the birches
Silver, River, Golden, Paper
each revealing their lessons in layers

I see the beauty of the earth
on display along the tree line
Brush strokes placed in wild precision
as nature basks in her own glory

I hear the song of forest birds
weaving mysteries among the branches
Speaking a language beyond my reach
rich in primal meaning

And I am left in awe
allowing the breeze to still my limbs
Knowing
that these are the moments
where life begins

(Painting "Birch Trees" by Andrea Rich)

Years
have the power
to change so much

But there are some things
that not even time itself
can touch

(Photo by Sara Wright)

And like the river
to the depths we fall
But oh how mighty
is the roar
of a wild
wandering soul
as layers of
the course unfold

(Photo by Joe Gall)

Give me the view of an open road
My untamed soul has places to go

(Photo by Matt Davis)

Through the process of growth
we obtain wisdom
Perspective
A wealth of tools
to aid in navigating the trials of life
But sometimes
the healthiest version of ourselves
is one which loses more than it gathers
For in order to find our greatest growth
we must unpack the bricks that weigh us down
Leave our burdens along the roadside
Scrape the scar tissue
from the flesh of our hearts
and be willing to discard the knives
that have been used upon our backs
Hurl them from our presence
Walk away
and continue on through life
as one who knows there is hidden worth
in mastering the art of traveling light

(Photo by Matt Davis)

A soul who loves to wander
should seek above all else
a sacred space within himself

So as his limbs are called to roam
his heart may always feel at home

(Photo by Joe Gall)

Every autumn
we yearn to learn again
about the process of release
and how we can come
to know ourselves
by allowing our burdens
to fall with the leaves

But this year
I have vowed to remember
that darkness has its season too

And there is much to learn
from the trees who bare the bitter cold
as they ache to teach the world
of the beauty found
in holding on
to the hope that spring
will bloom

(Photo by Matt Davis)

| 3 |

(Sketch by Katie Emery)

I am stripped
of the patchwork quilt
that had wrapped my frame
in the folds of autumn

Left to dress myself
in thicker layers
of fur lined blankets
and flannel cottons

(Painting by Shelby Kregel)

I have heard it said
that we should reach
for the stars

But I find that I
am most at home
with my feet exploring
the paths of the earth

And so for now
I think I shall seek
my peace there first

(Photo by Matt Davis)

No one understands
the beauty of the land
like the birds who stay behind

No one knows
where snow drifts blow
like the birds who roam
a winter sky

And although their wings
must bear the cold
what a blessing it must be

To be an audience
of the clouds
as nature adorns
herself in white

(Photo by Sara Wright)

Memories
of golden moments
are simply glimpses
the mind has chosen
to be frozen inside
the mirrors of time

(Photo by Joel Marotti)

I wish we could finally
normalize
the admittance that we all
have darkened corners
in our souls

Even the purest of hearts
hold memories
of a time they let
their morals fold

Even the most beautiful
of homes
hold spaces ruled
by spiders and ghosts

(Photo by Joe Gall)

May there be more
to your days
than shades of grey
May you fight your way
towards the light of the stars
and find your courage
in the void of darkness
wrapped in nothing
but your own arms

(Photo by Sara Wright)

| 4 |

(Sketch by Katie Emery)

Even the smallest
buds of warmth
bring forth a flush
upon my cheeks

A crescendo of color
begins to grow
as the chill is melted
from my bones

And I awake
to a brand new day
where the world has shed
a shade of grey

(Painting by Shelby Kregel)

My heart is craving wild days
The kind where my feet are free
to roam the wilderness in peace

No expectations
No limitations

A feral woman of the woods
listening to the wind for guidance
eating berries and naming falcons

(Body Painting by Kristen Zamora)

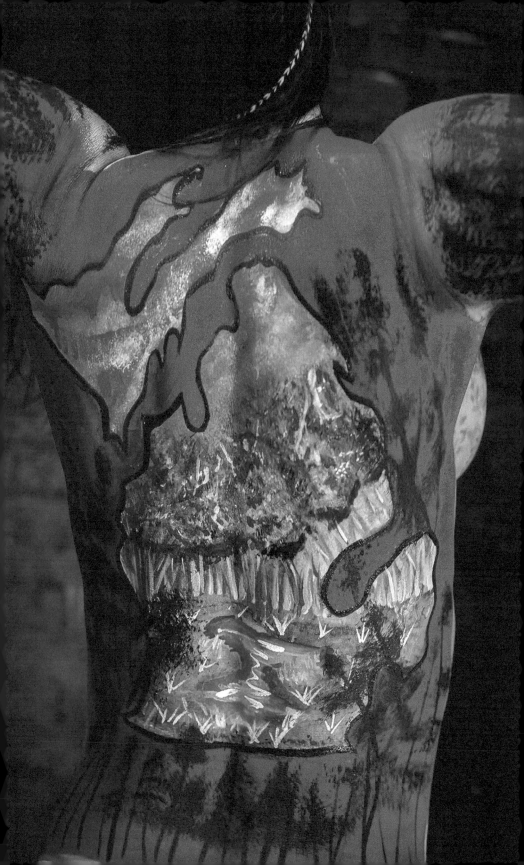

If only I could be
as profound as the sound
of a morning breeze
rustling its way amidst the trees
Perhaps the world
would remember me
as something worth experiencing

In the same way the Falcons
awake each day
and turn their gaze towards the east
to feast their senses upon
the horizon
and discover whatever
may come their way

(Drawing by Angel Portice)

I have learned more
from whispered lessons
of the wilderness
than I ever will
from a classroom ruled
by other humans

(Painting "Lupine Coast" by Kathleen Kalinowski)

I know how hard it feels
to have an open mind
But otherwise
I fear one day you may
discover
that over all this time
You have been confusing
safety nets with cages
And holding on
to windmill wings
that were never designed
to help you fly

(Paper Burning and Watercolor by Angel Portice)

Whatever you have faced
in the sunlight
you can conquer in the dark
For though the atmosphere
has shifted
Nothing has changed
about who you are

(Photo by Joel Marotti)

Connection
in its purest form
offers a glimpse
of the heart at ease

(Photo by Matt Davis)

We are bound to the salt of the earth
through a universal, connective design
and I cannot pretend to know the creator
nor the powers who have imagined time

But I do perceive a holy presence
when the storms that darken a pastel sky
bare strong resemblance to the light I find
behind the eyes of my own kind

And I do believe there is more to life
than the minds of men can comprehend

So somewhere in the realm
of truths my heart can understand
lay pathways leading towards the divine
and a trail of breadcrumbs she has left behind

(Photo by Joe Gall)

I am a wildflower
in the wind
Rooted to the hills
Dancing
despite the rocky terrain
Daring the sun
to watch me bloom
and feeling thirsty
for the rain

(Painting "Wildflowers" by Kathleen Kalinowski)

Even on the days I stand alone
deserted by the company of human kind
my soul is never left untethered

Always, I am anchored to the earth
These lungs are one with the breath of the wind
My heart at home in the ebb of tides

Even in times of ache and mourning
when I am lost amidst the crossroads of life
the paths before me hold precious sunlight

Always, the sky will grant me guidance
directing me towards a fate less taken
where I am loved by the rocks beneath my feet

And I am kept safe
by all that grows along the shore
where the million spirits of sand and soil
are touched by the greatness
of the lakes

(Painting "Steadfast" by Andrea Rich)

In the end
I hope to be remembered
as a woman who knew
her own depths
As a muse who planted roots
along the highest ledge

I pray they know my name
as one who flew despite the fall
and found her freedom
in the balance
of honoring both
her feathers and talons

(Body Painting of Wawatam Lighthouse by Kristen Zamora)

Meet The Artists

Kristen Zamora

Andrea Rich

Kathleen Kalinowski

Sara Wright

Matt Davis

Katie Emery

Joe Gall

Joel Marotti

Shelby Kregel

Angel Portice

Kristen Zamora (Adams)

Kristen Zamora is a proud momma, a professional face and body painter, healing facilitator and social activist. Kristen has worked on several independent films, theater performances, and has had her body paintings published in 7 different magazines, with the most recent being Bare Bones Magazine. Kristen is well known for her world wide healing body painting project, Embodied-Healing Through Body Art. Her healing body painting project, Embodied, won at Grand Rapids Michigan ArtPrize 2022. Embodied takes you through your story and identifies the elements that helped you through it. Kristen takes those elements of healing and paints your story on your body. Giving the opportunity to embody and honor your old story and scrub it away to rewrite a new one.

She is a certified Reiki practitioner, works with tuning forks and loves teaching others breath work. Kristen believes in empowering women through their stories, as well as the importance of getting back into your body and removing stigmas through art. Kristen uses the power of vulnerability and art to have hard conversations where conversation is needed. You can learn more about Kristen and her work at her website, www.kfxembodyart.com.

Andrea Rich

Andrea Rich is a self-taught oil artist from West Michigan. She creates impressionistic, brightly colored oil paintings inspired by nature. Her hope is to bring joy through her work and inspire others to follow their dreams. When she isn't painting, this wife and mother enjoys hanging out with her family and their dog Ruby. She also loves summer, gardening, and going to the beach! To see more of her work, you can find her on Instagram @inkedimpressionist or on Facebook @artbyandrearich.

Kathleen Kalinowski

Kathleen Kalinowski is a contemporary impressionist painter known for her poetic interpretations of the rural landscape. Her paintings explore the nuances of nature inspired by working outside on location, *en plein air* in all seasons. Her award winning work in oil and pastel has been accepted into many prestigious regional and national juried exhibitions, and numerous gallery and solo exhibits. Kathleen is an established artist who is widely collected in private and corporate collections. She is honored to be represented by three Michigan galleries. You can learn more about her incredible work by visiting her website at www.kathleenkalinowski.com.

Sara Wright

Photographer Sara Wright began her artistic career as a photographer at the Grand Hotel on Mackinac Island in 2006 while earning her BFA from Central Michigan University. Sara finds joy in capturing beautiful Mackinac Island from a romantic and vibrant perspective. Living and working on Mackinac Island year round provides endless inspiration for photographing the ever changing landscape of the seasons.

After working as a photographer for Grand Hotel for 15 years, Sara is now an independent freelance photographer and owner of It's Wonderful Photography on Mackinac Island - specializing in wedding, commercial and landscape photography.

You can follow Sara on Instagram @greendrinks and @itswonderfulphotography, or visit her website www.itswonderfulphotography.com.

Matt Davis

Matt Davis is a photographer from the Lansing area who operates under the name MAD Five O Photography. He has a natural eye for landscapes and strives to do things differently. He naturally gravitates towards different angles, moody edits and darker vibes. Although landscape photography is his passion, he also does portraits, family photos, lifestyle photos and branding. When he isn't taking pictures, you can find him drinking beer, playing music, being a dad and spending time outdoors (but only if it's warm!). He believes that photography is a unique art form that he is proud to call his craft.

You can find more of his work on his website www.madfiveophotography.com or on Instagram @mad_five_o_photography.

Katie Emery

Katie Emery is an artist and art educator in the mid-Michigan area. She holds a Bachelor of Arts degree from Trinity Christian College in art education and art history, and earned her Masters in Teaching and Curriculum from Michigan State University. With a passion for creating joy and adding glitter to everyday life, she creates everything from festive holiday tiaras to watercolors of Parisian cityscapes, but you will never find glitter in her art classroom. Katie has always been a maker, from a line of handmade greeting cards made in elementary school, to her current endeavor that fuses her love of fashion with art in her polymer clay jewelry. You can follow Katie on Instagram @KLE.make.

Joe Gall

Joe Gall (aka Camera Jesus) is a full time freelance photographer from the metro Detroit area who has been living out his passion for photography since he was young. He has a unique reputation for versatility; specializing in everything from stunning wildlife photography and outdoor adventure shots, to high profile concerts and even commercial photography for companies like Red Bull, Ford and Adidas. His talent has been showcased in magazines like Rolling Stone, Spin, and National Geographic.

While he often travels the world, capturing the magic of all different landscapes and lifestyles, Joe will always feel his deepest connection to Detroit, believing the city never runs out of things to photograph. He is also a proud father and avid adventure seeker.

You can find more of Joe's work on Instagram under @camera_jesus. He also has a website where you can buy some of his incredible work on print, at camerajesus.bigcartel.com.

Joel Marotti

Joel Marotti is an outdoor enthusiast and photographer from West Michigan. Growing up near Lake Michigan, he developed a deep love for the outdoors, which eventually led him to become interested in photography as a way to document his own travels. Today, he uses his imagery to share the incredible beauty found throughout Michigan and beyond. With a passion for nature and a keen eye for detail, Joel captures stunning images of landscapes, the night sky, and outdoor adventures that inspire and captivate his audience. You can find him on Instagram under @nat_geo_vibes.

Shelby Kregel

Shelby Kregel is a watercolor and acrylic artist from Grand Rapids. She loves painting landscapes, abstracts, wildlife, and anything floral. She lives with her husband and three darling little girls- Daisy, Maple and Rosie. When not painting, their family is often headed to the beach, or finding a trail to explore.

You can find more of Shelby's work on Instagram under @shelbykregel or on her Etsy shop at Etsy.com/shop/shelbykregel.

Angel Portice

Angel Abbs-Portice is a self taught realist artist, living in Pickford, Michigan. After having great middle school and high school art teachers, she taught herself all different forms of art. When she couldn't find anyone to teach her to wood burn, or glass etch, she researched and taught herself how to do them. She then tried to take them to the next level. She is inspired by nature and animals. She loves the detail work in art and prides herself on capturing the soul of whatever she is working on.

Her works are now mostly purchased on consignment specifically for her customers. Angel's art has been featured in multiple art museum openings and covered in several newspapers and magazines. She creates awards for horse and dog groups on a regular basis. Her art has been sold all over the United States, Canada, Europe and Africa. You can find Angel on Facebook under Arc Angel Artistry.

For more poetry
by Jennifer Gordon
visit jennifergordonpoetry.com
or follow her on Instagram
@jennifergordonpoetry

Her first two published collections
Poems To Read In The Rain
and
The Nature Of Night
are both available worldwide

CPSIA information can be obtained
at www.ICGtesting.com
Printed in the USA
BVHW011235150623
666005BV00008B/580